The HAPPINESS Diary

Brimming with creative inspiration, how-to projects, and useful information to enrich your everyday life, Quarto Knows is a favorite destination for those pursuing their interests and passions. Visit our site and dig deeper with our books into your area of interest: Quarto Creates, Quarto Cooks, Quarto Homes, Quarto Lives, Quarto Drives, Quarto Explores, Quarto Gifts, or Quarto Kids.

© 2019 Quarto Publishing Group USA Inc.
Text © 2019 Barbara Ann Kipfer

First Published in 2019 by Fair Winds Press, an imprint of The Quarto Group, 100 Cummings Center, Suite 265-D, Beverly, MA 01915, USA. T (978) 282-9590 F (978) 283-2742 QuartoKnows.com

Fair Winds Press titles are also available at discount for retail, wholesale, promotional, and bulk purchase. For details, contact the Special Sales Manager by email at specialsales@quarto.com or by mail at The Quarto Group, Attn: Special Sales Manager, 100 Cummings Center, Suite 265-D, Beverly, MA 01915, USA.

23 22 21 20 19   1 2 3 4 5
ISBN: 978-1-59233-858-0
Digital edition published in 2019
eISBN: 978-1-63159-625-4

Library of Congress Cataloging-in-Publication Data
Kipfer, Barbara Ann, author.
The happiness diary / Barbara A Kipfer.
ISBN 9781592338580 (trade pbk.) | ISBN 9781631596254 (eISBN)
Subjects: LCSH: Happiness.
LCC BF575.H27 K534 2019 | DDC 152.4/2--dc23
LCCN 2018044043

Design: Joanne Hus
Cover Image: Trina Dalziel
Page Layout: Joanne Hus
Illustration: Trina Dalziel

Printed in China

The HAPPINESS *Diary*

Practice Living Joyfully

Barbara Ann Kipfer

FAIR WINDS

CONTENTS

Introduction 6

1. Your Definition of Happiness 8

2. Methodologies 34

3. Focus on the Present Moment 46

4. Secrets to Mindfulness 82

5. Capturing the Little Things 98

6. How to Compile Your Own Collection 122

7. Changing Your Brain 134

8. Sharing Happiness 150

About the Author 160

Introduction

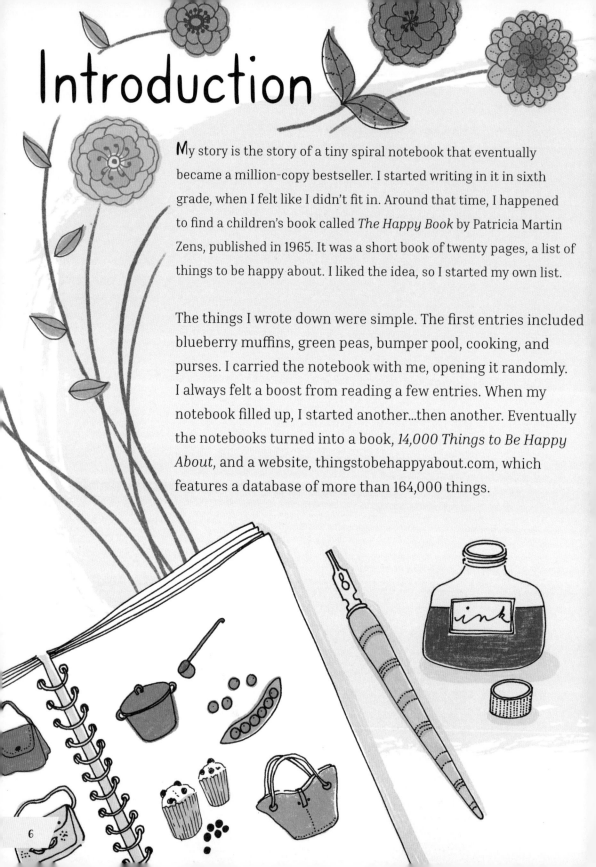

My story is the story of a tiny spiral notebook that eventually became a million-copy bestseller. I started writing in it in sixth grade, when I felt like I didn't fit in. Around that time, I happened to find a children's book called *The Happy Book* by Patricia Martin Zens, published in 1965. It was a short book of twenty pages, a list of things to be happy about. I liked the idea, so I started my own list.

The things I wrote down were simple. The first entries included blueberry muffins, green peas, bumper pool, cooking, and purses. I carried the notebook with me, opening it randomly. I always felt a boost from reading a few entries. When my notebook filled up, I started another...then another. Eventually the notebooks turned into a book, *14,000 Things to Be Happy About*, and a website, thingstobehappyabout.com, which features a database of more than 164,000 things.

Most importantly, those simple notebooks turned into a practice, a way to cultivate happiness and mindfulness. And with this journal, you can use it, too.

Mindfulness is an important factor, a first step, but mindfulness alone is not enough. Savoring and ingraining the good things you experience grows you a garden from which you will be able to pick flowers when challenges come. It is long-term, resilient happiness inside of you that does not rely on obtaining stuff or on outward circumstances being perfect. This practice is valuable in good times and bad times, a constant companion to help navigate the ups and downs of life.

Let's get started!

Your Definition of Happiness

Defining happiness is like defining art, love, or another abstract concept: It's hard to do! The exercises in this section will help you work through your personal definition.

WISH LIST

Make a list of things you want—the "if only I had/was/could" list. Come back to this page in one month and again in one year, and make a new list each time. What did you achieve from the original list? What sort of achievements affected your happiness? Did you feel the way you thought you would? Or did you just replace the list with a new list?

TODAY'S DATE:

1/12/20

ONE MONTH:

Real estate agent

ONE YEAR:

Sell a house

CAN'T LIVE WITHOUT IT

Make a list of things, including people,
you believe you cannot live without.

family

cat

handbag with contents

keepsakes

My mom + dad
kerry, Michael
Andrew, christian
Lauren, lulu, my
house, my friends,
music

Look at the list gently, without judging. Can you imagine
changing the list, simplifying your needs and desires?

MIND~MAPPING HAPPINESS

Set a timer for one minute. Before it chimes, write words or phrases that come to mind when you see the word "happiness." Aim for ten. Do this freely and don't judge which words come to you. You can add more lines leading off of your answers, or connect them, if you like.

Happiness

Look at the associations you made
to the word happiness. What do they
say about you? What are the obvious
patterns? Do you have control over many of the
associations, or do you feel that they are out of your control?

HAPPINESS ASSOCIATION

Make a list of the first fifty words or phrases that come to mind when you think of happiness.

1

2

3

4

5

6

7

8

9

10

11

12

13

14

15

16

17

18

19

20

21

22

23

24

25

26

27

28

29

30

31

32

33

34

35

36

37

38

39

40

41

42

43

44

45

46

47

48

49

50

Over the next few days, turn to this list when things are going badly, and read a few words. You can start to train your mind to think in these terms more often.

WHAT DEFINES YOU?

Write down ten words that define you. Names don't count.

1

2

3

4

5

6

7

8

9

10

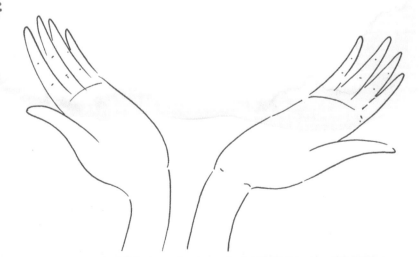

Use this page
to journal or
to write a poem
using each of
the ten words
you came
up with.

YOUR CORE VALUES

Make a list, from your heart, of your top six core values. Take your time, and don't worry about what other people would think of your list.

compassion

creativity

fitness

education

kindness

1

2

3

4

5

6

YOUR CORE VALUES: ACTION PLAN

Transfer each of your core values from the previous page to one of these boxes. Think of a way—large or small—that you can live that value on a daily basis, and write it in the box. Then, and this is the hard part, put it into action. It may take several tries to make your action a habit, but keep trying until you do.

VALUE:

ACTION:

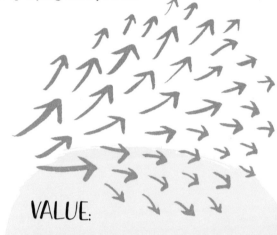

VALUE:

ACTION:

VALUE:

ACTION:

VALUE:

ACTION:

VALUE:

ACTION:

VALUE:

ACTION:

MEANING, PLEASURE, AND STRENGTH

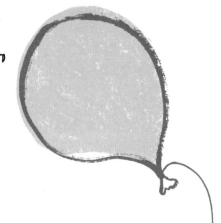

WHAT GIVES YOU MEANING?

Do you see any trends in your answers to these questions? Where do they overlap? What does that tell you about what kind of work and play make you happiest?

WHAT GIVES YOU PLEASURE?

WHAT ARE YOUR STRENGTHS?

FIND YOUR PASSION

List five things that you're passionate about.

1
....

2
....

3
....

4
....

5
....

WHAT INTEREST, PASSION, OR DESIRE ARE YOU
MOST AFRAID OF ADMITTING TO YOURSELF AND OTHERS?

WHAT WOULD YOU DO IF YOU KNEW YOU COULD NOT FAIL?

WHO DO YOU KNOW THAT'S DOING SOMETHING YOU'D LIKE TO DO?

WHAT'S STOPPING YOU FROM MOVING FORWARD
WITH EXPLORING YOUR PASSION?

WHAT WOULD YOU REGRET NOT HAVING DONE
IF YOUR LIFE WAS ENDING?

IS THIS WHAT I REALLY WANT?

Close your eyes and take three deep breaths. When you're ready, set a timer for ten minutes. Until it chimes, free-write without stopping or editing about the things you really, really want. Include things you already have in your life and things you want to bring to it—large or small.

LIFE MAP

WHERE DO YOU SEE YOURSELF IN FIVE YEARS?
WHERE DO YOU SEE YOURSELF IN TEN YEARS?

DID YOU BASE YOUR ANSWERS ON YOUR CORE VALUES, YOUR
PASSIONS, YOUR SKILLS, AND/OR YOUR INTERESTS AND HOBBIES?

"All of humanity's problems
stem from man's inability
to sit quietly in a room alone."

—Blaise Pascal

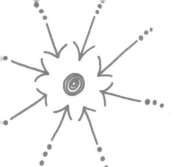

Make a pie chart that reflects the major constituents of your life—such as work, education, family, creativity, and community—and how much time and effort they take up in your life right now.

Make a pie chart that reflects what you would like the major constituents of your life to be in ten years.

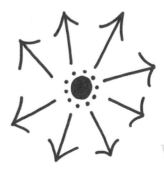

START A GRATITUDE JOURNAL

Put a journal on your nightstand. Each night before nodding off, write the numbers 1 through 5 on a page, and then fill in the blanks with things you are grateful for. You will begin to look for things throughout your day to write down each night. This practice shifts your focus away from what is wrong in your life to what is right and beautiful and kind in the world. This exercise is a self-fulfilling one. When you begin to think about the things you are grateful for, you become more grateful for them. As you focus on both big and small things to be thankful for, soon, your world is filled with gratifying thoughts and experiences.

Another way to do this is to keep a gratitude journal in the kitchen and jot down a few things as you sip your first cup of coffee or tea in the morning. This is a lovely ritual for beginning your day on a positive note. If you set your alarm ten minutes earlier to do this exercise, you will have a better day.

the time to exercise physically and mentally

companionship and friendship

the beauty and playfulness of a gray tiger cat

learning something new

a menu with everything spelled correctly

Methodologies

What is the best way to start on a happiness path? This book uses several methods, including list-making, journal entries, writing prose, mind-mapping, and drawing. We'll try them in this section so you can decide which ones suit you best.

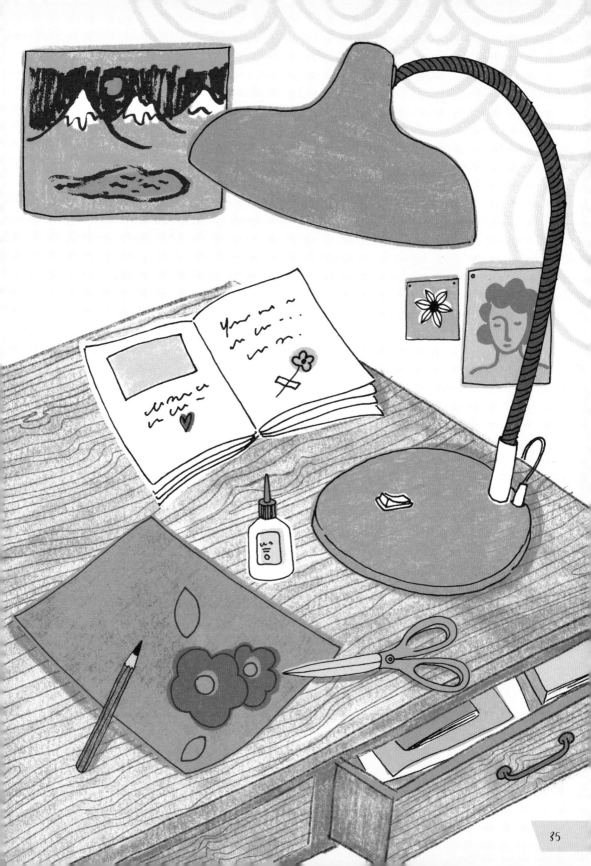

MAKE LISTS

Every night before you go to bed
for the next week, write down
five things you're grateful for.

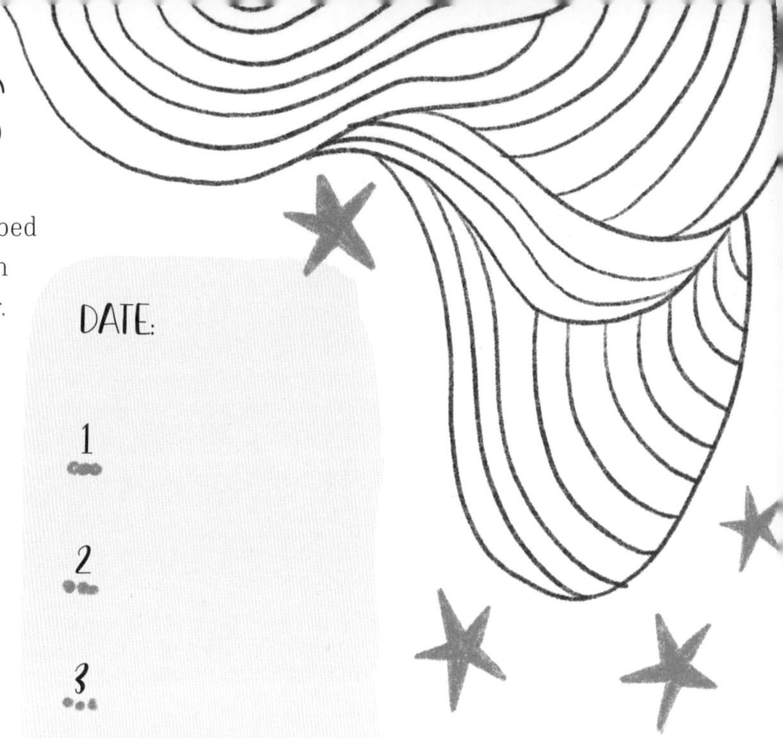

DATE:

1

2

3

4

5

DATE:

1

2

3

4

5

DATE:

1

2

3

4

5

DATE:

1

2

3

4

5

DATE:

1

2

3

4

5

DATE:

1

2

3

4

5

DATE:

1

2

3

4

5

Lists offer order, real or perceived, in a chaotic world. They can be fun, inspiring, motivational, and useful. If this list-making exercise appeals to you, consider getting yourself a special notebook just for keeping lists.

JOURNAL

In this space, write about a mundane task or errand in detail, as if you were describing a major project. After all, each detail represents some precious moments of your time on Earth. Focus on just one thing at a time. Make sure you are not thinking about all the other things you could be doing and accomplishing while you are working on this task. Appreciate the task(s) you have accomplished while describing them.

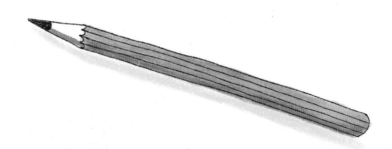

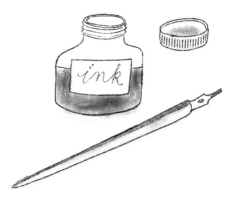

Journaling can help you work through problems, increase mindfulness, keep you focused on your goals, assist your memory, strengthen your self-discipline, and stimulate your creativity. If this journaling exercise appeals to you, get yourself a journal (physical or electronic, private or online) and write in it every day for three weeks. Date each entry and keep your finished journals somewhere safe so you can reread them.

WRITE CREATIVELY

Open a dictionary and choose a word at random—or choose your favorite word.
Use it in the first line of a poem you write for yourself or someone else.

Creative writing can mean poetry, stories, novels, screenplays, essays, flash fiction, and more. It can help you capture and savor things to be happy about, work through problems and difficult times, and set goals and new directions. Set aside some time and get started writing what you've always wanted to write.

MAKE MIND MAPS

Write something you want to create—a creative goal—in the rectangle below. Brainstorm ideas for how to accomplish it; write each one down around the rectangle and connect it with a line. Add further thoughts supporting those ideas, if you need to. Feel free to use multiple colors of pen or pencil. And feel free to get messy—sometimes a supporting thought may need to connect to more than one idea.

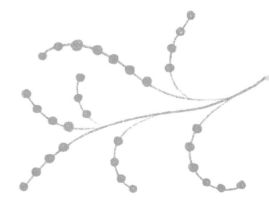

Mind-mapping is a highly effective way of getting information in and out of your brain. It lets you "map out" the ideas or concepts in your mind. If mind-mapping appeals to you, get yourself a blank sketchbook for making maps. Or go all in and hang a big roll of white butcher paper on your wall!

ART JOURNAL

Find an old photograph of your family or friends that is connected to an important story. Make a copy of it and paste or tape it to this page. Using the rest of the space, tell the story with words and/or images.

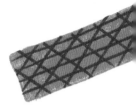

If art journaling appeals to you, get an unlined journal
suitable to your favorite media. Draw, paint, collage,
write, or do whatever else helps you express yourself.

Focus on the Present Moment

The practice of finding and savoring things to be happy about happens in the present moment. This chapter offers exercises to practice doing just that, and its "wake-up calls" will be helpful to you throughout your everyday life.

TAKE A MOMENT

Put aside some time during the day to focus on your senses. Slow down, center yourself, and take stock of each sense in turn. Notice the smell of your first cup of coffee, the soft feel of your bathrobe after a shower. Be fully present—no past, no future, no turmoil. What did you notice?

DEVELOPING MINDFULNESS

POP QUIZ!

Make a list of things you paid attention to yesterday. Answer these questions as thoroughly as you can. Did you have any moments of pure awareness? What did you do that you would like to do again?

fresh flowers in the lobby of an office

a rerun of your favorite TV show

the greeting from your pet after you've been away all day

making it through the green light

getting the last copy of the newspaper from the store

a bathroom when you need it

the luxury of a shower

a worth-the-money meal

smooth travel

standing in front of a fan

USE MEMORIES TO GROW YOUR HAPPINESS

List the top ten ways you usually seek happiness. These are memories.

1

2

3

4

5

6

7

8

9

10

watch a favorite TV show

listen to music

practice yoga

eat a pint of ice cream

read a magazine

go on a media fast

read an encyclopedia article

walk in the rain

take up kayaking

perform a Japanese tea ceremony

decide not to answer the phone

Now draw on your happy memories, but think outside your box. What are ten new methods you could try to seek happiness?

1

2

3

4

5

6

7

8

9

10

MAKE A WISH

Write down the things you have always wanted to do. Prioritize in each section, if you like, by what is feasible in your life. In the second column, write down the first step toward making that wish come true.

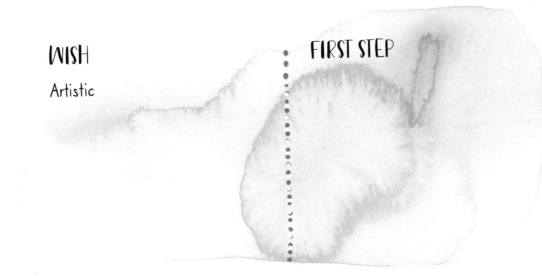

WISH

Artistic

FIRST STEP

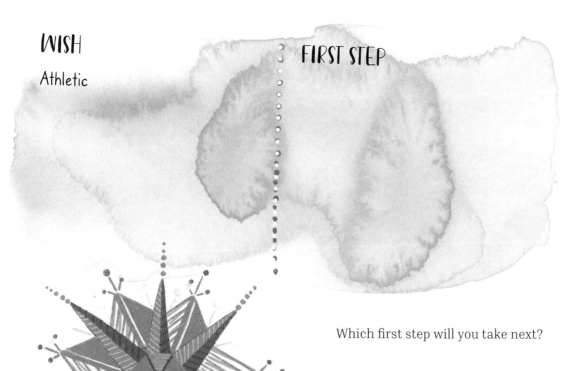

WISH

Athletic

FIRST STEP

Which first step will you take next?

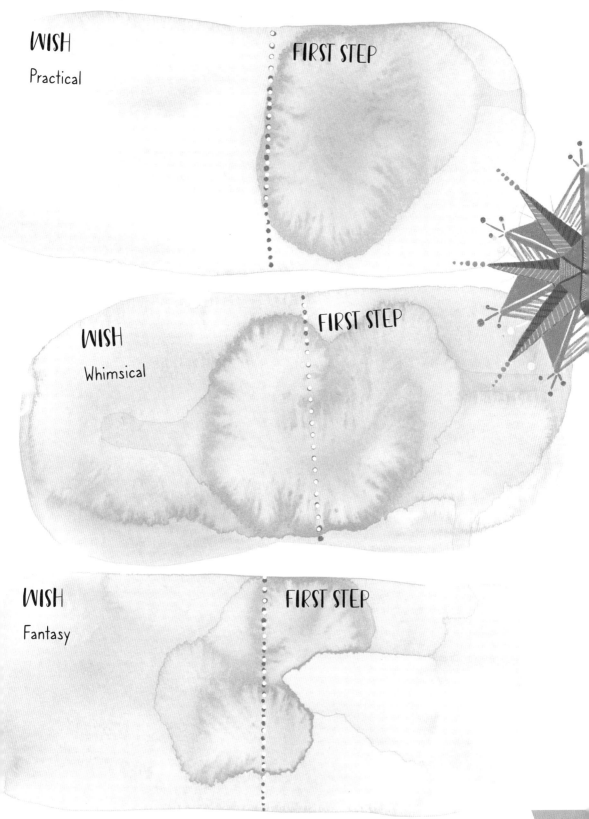

WISH
Practical

FIRST STEP

WISH
Whimsical

FIRST STEP

WISH
Fantasy

FIRST STEP

WHERE ARE YOU RIGHT NOW?

Write about where you are NOW in your life. What events mark it off: spouse/partner, kids, parents, school, career? How far back does this period reach? What have been the main characteristics of this recent period?

Do you like NOW? Would you prefer a drastic change? Do you see a major change happening soon? If your NOW is not what you had hoped it would be, do you feel that you have the power and courage to change it? Do you feel that you have to stick it out in your NOW for a while? If you enjoy your NOW, how can you maintain it?

"Attitude is a choice. Happiness is a choice. Optimism is a choice. Kindness is a choice. Giving is a choice. Respect is a choice. Whatever choice you make makes you. Choose wisely."

—Roy T. Bennett

QUIT STRUGGLING WITH TIME

Describe your relationship with time. Do you give it too much power? You can ease your struggle with time by learning time-management skills. It's mainly about setting priorities and making the solid decision that you do indeed have time for what is important. You can say "no" to the extraneous, and learn how to graciously extract yourself from people and situations that should not take time away from you.

"One always has time enough, if only one applies it well."

—*Johann W. von Goethe*

FIND HAPPINESS IN THE MUNDANE

Yes, there they are again, the dishes. Didn't you just do them? Okay, not a big deal—let's just do them and get it over with.

Wait. How much of your day do you spend getting it over with?

Pick a mundane activity that usually puts you on autopilot. This week, as you do it, focus on it. Stay in the moment by breathing and slowing down and focusing on the activity instead of either zoning out or following your monkey mind wherever it takes you. Enjoy the struggle.

How did it go? What did you notice?

CLEAN THINGS OUT

Cleaning up the clutter, getting rid of trash, and donating unused items can bring much happiness. It is also a great present-moment activity. Use this page to map out all the places you need to clean out, both physical and mental. Draw receptacles where the trash goes. A key ingredient to living a happier life is simplifying it.

If possible, be generous in donating items to worthy causes. Give things away that you will truly never use again, and take a moment to understand how much you are going to enrich someone else's life with your gift.

NEWNESS

After cleaning out, it is good to examine our fascination with new things. Newness has a way of offering us hope. With awareness, you can see this. Each moment is a fresh start, open to new opportunities, new personal growth. If you practice treating each moment as new and special, it changes everything. You look at the present moment as a beginner, as a tiny child. Looking at every moment as if for the first time helps you appreciate change, which is never-ending. Spend a few minutes writing about your appreciation for new things that are not stuff: new people, experiences, and ideas.

NEWNESS CHALLENGE

Every day for the next month, make an effort to learn something new every day, even if it is something small.

DATE   WHAT I LEARNED

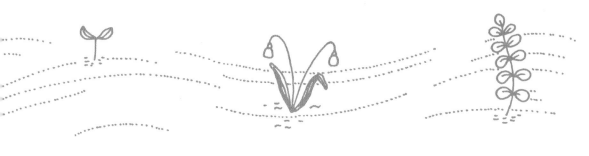

DATE   WHAT I LEARNED

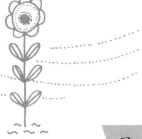

GO NATURAL

Spend some time outside and really pay attention to nature. What do you observe?

Find or create something you can tend to and nurture—flowers, herbs, an entire garden, even a pet. What is it?

Come back to this page after one month. How is it going? What have you learned?

START SOMETHING POSITIVE

Make a list of cool projects you could start—or get back to. They can be large or small, so long as you can do them, and they can be completed. You want the sense of accomplishment!

 1

 2

3

4

5

Now pick one of the projects and do it. When you're finished, come back to this page and journal about how it made you feel.

Make a second list of projects with other people in mind—perhaps making dinner for someone, volunteering for beach or park cleanup, or running errands for someone who can't.

1

2

3

4

5

Do one of the projects, come back to this page, and journal about how it made you feel.

ADD SOME ADVENTURE

What's on your bucket list? Keeping in mind that happiness is often found in experiences rather than physical goods—especially if those experiences are social, memorable, educational, adventurous, or altruistic—make a list of adventures you want to embark on. You can keep coming back to this list, adding to it and crossing things off for years, but for now, pick a line item and start making plans.

FEED YOUR MIND

Feed your mind with reading, learning, music, and creative activities. Use this page to make a list of the mind-nourishing activities you want to explore and check them off when you do.

THE ART OF LOUNGING

Doing nothing (without feeling guilty) is a skill we need to learn. At the end of the day, it is important to take your mind off things and let your thoughts idle. Your cognitive self needs to slow down before you can get a good night's sleep.

For this exercise, get into a comfortable position and stay put until your brain settles. Be patient and savor the silence. No matter what calls to you—something you forgot to fix, the text message coming in, the pull to write down a list on a Post-it note—just stay put. You are restless and it takes time to quiet down your mental activity and manage your restlessness. Put your conscious mind on sabbatical. Stay still as long as you can.

How did it go?

Challenge yourself to do
this nightly for at least
a week. What effect
does it have on you?

TRAINING YOUR ATTENTION

Look around the room or space where you're reading this and pick a thing—ideally something you normally take for granted. Use all of this space to describe and journal about it.

"Compose yourself in stillness, draw your attention inward, and devote your mind to the Self. The wisdom you seek lies within."

—Bhagavad Gita

LIVE EACH DAY

Journal about today. What could you choose to do to bring more meaning and purpose into your life on this day? What should you think and do to make yourself and others smile, feel joy, and be happy? How can you make the world a better place because you have this day to live?

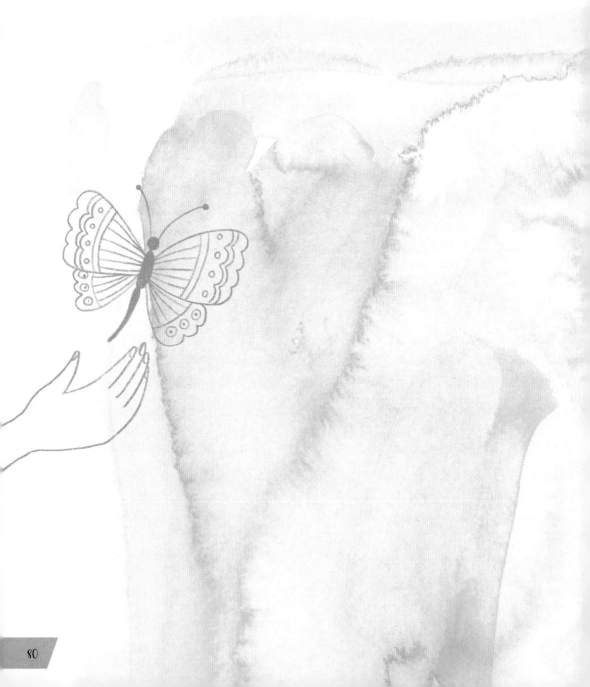

Welcome each new day
with a mindful smile for
each breath you take. Ask
that you may live each
moment with compassion
and awareness. Ask that
you may walk on a path
of peace and do no harm.
Ask that you become
more aware. Each day,
spend some time in quiet
contemplation of your own
wealth of knowledge and
talents. Live to the fullest.

Secrets to Mindfulness

Mindfulness is attending to NOW. Being mindful calms you, makes your mind still. You can use your determination to increase your mindfulness from moment to moment. Further, you can train yourself to see more and experience more happy moments.

TRAIN YOUR SELF~MINDFULNESS

Make a list of your personal strengths and talents. Can you open your mind to see some hidden abilities that you have not admitted to having? Examine each strength for your level of excitement, yearning, even joy that you feel about it. Jot down some notes on how you can use it as frequently as possible.

STRENGTH

HOW I FEEL ABOUT IT

HOW I CAN USE IT

· ·

· ·

· ·

· ·

· ·

· ·

· ·

· ·

· ·

· ·

· ·

· ·

· ·

· ·

"To live means to
be aware, joyously,
drunkenly,
serenely, divinely
aware.**"**

—*Henry Miller*

DAILY MINDFULNESS

At the beginning of each week, choose a simple regular activity that you usually do on autopilot. Resolve to make that activity into a reminder to wake up your mindfulness. You could choose making tea or coffee, shaving, bathing, watering the plants, turning on lights, etc. Resolve to pause for a few seconds each time, before you start the activity. Then carry it out with gentle and complete attention. Try to bring mindfulness to this act each time. Each week, add another activity to daily mindfulness, cultivating it as a new habit.

I am becoming happier.

the core of my being is at peace.

each experience I have is an opportunity for greater growth.

there are no mistakes, only lessons

I forgive all who have hurt me.

I forgive myself for all I have hurt.

I go forth in love and peace.

I send loving thoughts to all living beings

WEEK OF (DATE)

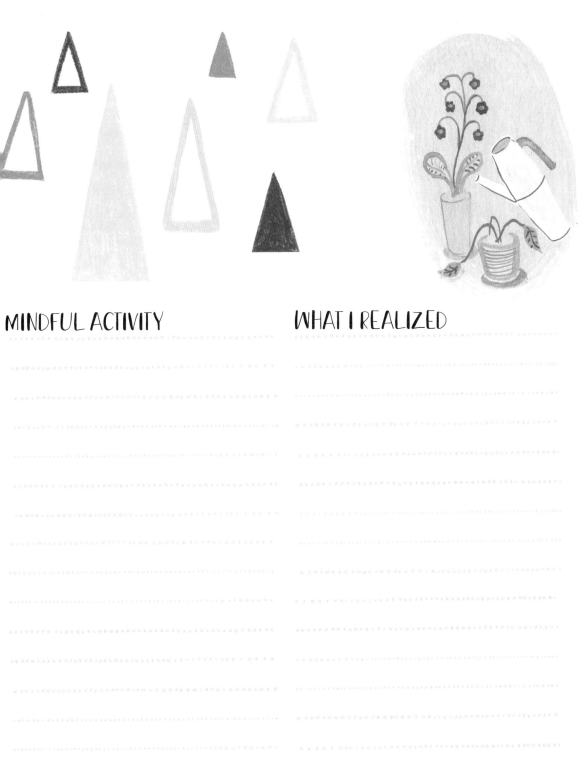

MINDFUL ACTIVITY

WHAT I REALIZED

REMEMBER THAT CONVERSATION?

Think of a recent conversation you had with someone and write down what you remember as the main points. Identify the motivations or intentions behind things you said and note the responses to or effects of your words.

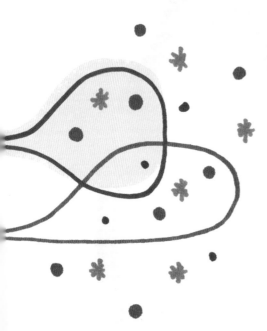

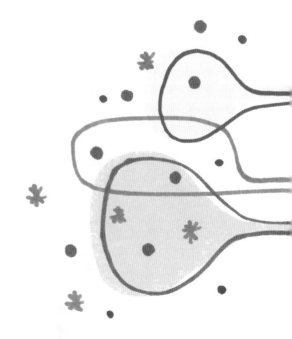

DIGITAL DETOX

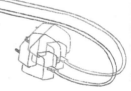

Spend a day taking note of the small sounds of technology you probably tune out most of the time—computer, the refrigerator running, the dishwasher chugging, video game songs and blips, the spinning of the washing machine, etc. Use this space to record them.

Can you do anything to reduce the overall background noise in your life, perhaps by turning machines off when you aren't using them?

If you can, schedule a digital detox for a day. Refrain from using electronic devices such as smartphones and computers. It's an opportunity to reduce stress and focus on true social interaction and connection with nature—so bonus points if you can do it somewhere outside and with friends.

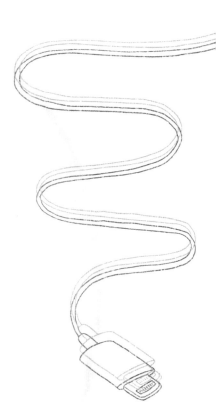

SAVOR

Every day for the next week, be sure to savor at least two experiences (for example, your morning coffee, the sun on your face as you walk to your car, or the sound of your child's voice). Totally immerse yourself in the moment and try not to think, just sense. Spend at least two to three minutes savoring each experience. Understand the impact that this savoring is having on your life. Become aware of this new feeling and enjoy it.

DATE	FIRST EXPERIENCE	SECOND EXPERIENCE

DATE	FIRST EXPERIENCE	SECOND EXPERIENCE

> "Seize every second of your life and savor it. Value your present moments."
>
> —Wayne Dyer

CELEBRATE!

We're used to celebrating birthdays and holidays, but take this opportunity to think smaller for a little bit. Make a list of some of the small occurrences and victories in your life you could be celebrating. Then get to it!

half-birthdays

gray hairs

Sweetest Day, the fall version of Valentine's Day

good food from the earth

your pet's birthday, even though they have no idea what is going on

community

surviving the dentist

THE BEST THINGS IN LIFE

One of the benefits of mindfulness is that it helps you notice the little things in life—many of which are covered by the adage, "the best things in life are free." Use this space to make a list of some of the best things in your life that are free—and include activities you like to do (or would like to try), too.

hiking the local park

stargazing

joking with sister

tennis with neighbor

Capturing the Little Things

Where should you be looking for happiness? It happens in your mind when you are in the moment, accepting it without wishing it to be otherwise, being mindful of the whole of life. This chapter will move around through various aspects of everyday life and help you see the possibilities for appreciation, gratitude, and simple happiness.

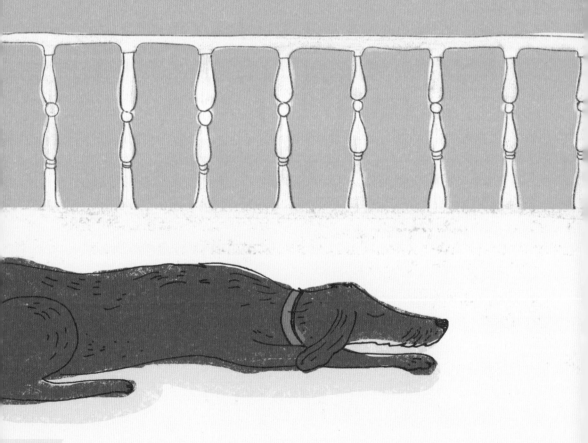

YOUR ENVIRONMENT

Spend some time sitting in, walking around, and truly appreciating your living space. Don't look for things that are wrong or things you want to fix; look at it for what it is right now. Make a list of things you are happy about in it. Consider the convenience you have, the comforts you take for granted, and even what other family members or pets enjoy.

a clear view of seasonally
changing nature

your favorite books in the bookcase

the reliability of appliances
like the refrigerator

a place to park your car

the comforting sound
of a wind chime

a dictionary by the bed

watching a movie in
your living room

a blanket spread out on the
ground to watch the stars

answering machines
and caller ID

the security offered by
a rubber bath mat

candles lit for dinnertime

the art of napkin folding

garbage-pickup day

knowing where (practically)
everything is

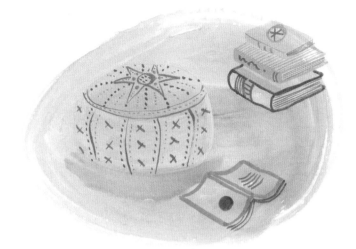

YOUR WORK

Do the same for your work life. Forget about the stressful aspects for the moment and make a list of the positives.

being part of a team project

how your work benefits others

the music you play at work

effective problem-solving

"To love what you do and feel that it matters —how could anything be more fun?**"**

—*Katharine Graham*

DREAM JOURNAL

Leave a pen and this book, open to this page, next to your bed. Before you go to sleep, spend a minute or two thinking about dreaming. Say to yourself, "I will remember my dreams" and repeat it several times. If a dream awakens you, write it down here.

When you wake up in the morning, resist jumping out of bed. Try to lie still and stay sleepy. The best time to remember your dreams is when you first wake up. What is rolling about in your head? Is there an image? a feeling? words? As you lie still, bits of your dreams may start to come back. Write down anything you can remember. Repeat this for several nights.

Are there any patterns to your dreams?

THAT'S FASCINATING

When you happen across an interesting piece of information or an idea you want to remember, use this page to write it down. This lets you free your mind from it—and when you combine it with the previous and future things you've noted, you may make even more interesting connections.

CAPTURE THE MOMENT

Spend a few minutes observing all the details of the present moment. Use every sense—sight, sound, smell, touch, and taste. Write down as much as you can.

Repeat on another day.

Are there patterns to your observations?
Senses you tend to ignore or rely on?

HAPPY BOOSTS

There are a lot of little things you can do to boost your happiness. If you are a commuter, a simple happy boost may be an audiobook or podcast for the car ride. If you work from home, it might be some stretches and a cup of coffee at 10 a.m. If you are a stay-at-home parent, it might be the twenty minutes you take for meditation after the kids go to bed. Whatever it is should add to your pleasure and fulfillment, nurturing calmness or patience, or general happiness. Use this space to make a list of simple happy boosts you can add to your life. Ideally, they should require few or no material resources.

do a relaxation exercise

go for a walk

read an interesting article

do some creative writing

meditate for twenty minutes

DRAWING ON HAPPINESS

Fill this page with drawings of things, large or small, that you are happy about.

PASTIMES AND HOBBIES

WHAT MAKES A HOBBY REWARDING FOR YOU?

take an art course

join a knitting group

become part of a
Wednesday-matinee
movie club

sign up for that
cooking class

play golf

hike

take yourself out for
a meal once a week
all by yourself

go to a bookstore to
browse after work or
on the weekend

WHAT TYPES OF HOBBIES DO YOU DO NOW? WHAT WERE YOUR PAST ACTIVITIES?

MAKE A LIST OF PASTIMES AND HOBBIES THAT YOU WOULD LIKE TO TRY.

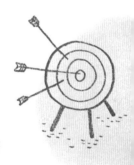

SIMPLE PLEASURES

You don't have to wait for the weekend or retirement to be happy. One way to bring the sense that you're enjoying your life to every day is to focus on the simple pleasures. Make a list of day-to-day things you can seek out, cultivate, and savor.

Some things you try may seem indulgent at first, but what are you waiting for? Don't you deserve happiness right now? What if you took the time to carefully arrange some fresh flowers, or drank your cup of coffee in the sun on the porch? What if you stopped for five minutes to pet a purring cat? Putting simple pleasures into your life and appreciating ones that just happen really brings happiness to your day.

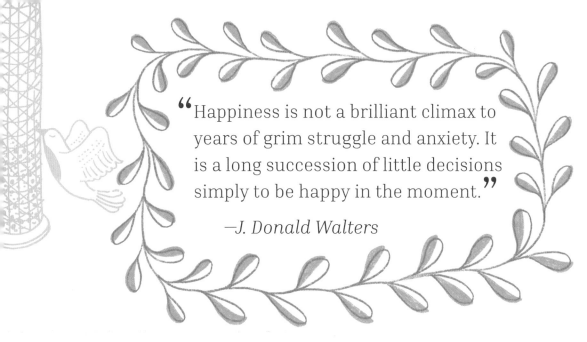

"Happiness is not a brilliant climax to years of grim struggle and anxiety. It is a long succession of little decisions simply to be happy in the moment."

—*J. Donald Walters*

SENSES OF PLEASURE

Next time you're having a happy experience, stop and focus on it. How does it look, sound, smell, feel, and taste? Later, journal about it here, describing it in as much detail as possible. Repeat with five to six experiences.

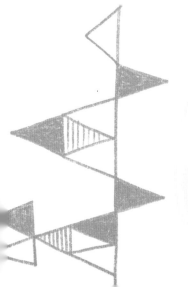

THINGS TO BE HAPPY ABOUT

Use this page to list things that make you happy. Include big things as they come to you, but pay particular attention to the little things that make your day incrementally brighter as you encounter them.

How to Compile Your Own Collection

Get yourself a notebook and decide the best way for you to keep track of it. Maybe it will go on your bedside table to be checked in with at night; maybe it will fit in your purse or pocket. Write something that makes you happy in it every day. This chapter will get you started finding places to pay attention.

PEOPLE

As people, we need people. Each of us has known extraordinary people, read and heard about them . . . and there will be more. Add people to your list who have admirable qualities and/or achievements. When people who had an impact on your life pass away, make sure they are on your list so you will have a way to remember them forever.

Octavia Butler

Thich Nhat Hanh

Joan Walsh Anglund

Robert Ballard

AA Milne

Grandmaster Flash

Sting

PLACES

There are places you have been, but even more that you are fascinated with. Documentaries, travelogues, books, magazines, movies, and television can certainly provide you with glimpses of other places so fascinating that you feel you are there. Add these places to your list.

When you do this, describe the details of a place, as if you were there. This exercise shows how words can take you places and allow you to experience things in a way that makes you feel happy. It is not necessary to actually visit these places. Reading or writing about different locales can offer you all kinds of happy moments.

Even more important, however, be where you are. See the details. Write them down.

THINGS

You don't need *things* to be happy, of course. Happiness is housed in your mind. But looking at images and artwork and reading about things can help you find things to add to your happiness list.

the teeth of a Scotch tape dispenser taking tiny bites of the cellophane until it completely lets go

field guides kept in the car

art gallery exhibits

Christmas trees behind half-drawn curtains

a north country fish fry

a reddish glow in the sky two hours after sunlight

a snapshot of a time period and a class of people

souffles on a lovely Sunday morning

BOOKS

Add the books that have changed your life to your list. Include the books that you feel people simply must read, or their lives will somehow be diminished. Include the books that you felt like you were watching as you read them. Respect the power of reading to shape your life and your world.

What books made you feel that you were not alone in the world? What books made you feel that there was someone else like you, who faced the same fears, the same confusions, the same grief, the same joys? What books took place in time periods or places that you would like to visit? What books challenged your core belief system? What books made you cry or laugh out loud?

EVENTS

Add your life's events and stepping-stones to the list.

Begin with "I remember," and write down lots of good memories. Don't be concerned with when the event happened, or trying to keep them in any specific order. Go for names, places, events, etc. Include as much detail as you can. Reliving these experiences will bring good feelings from the past into the present.

Are there patterns? Do your list's stepping-stones focus on certain areas or places? Are these the areas that you see as the source of your happiness? Does the list make you proud? Does it inspire you?

There is a part of each of us that needs to interact with things in the past. Though we aim to center ourselves in the present moment, we can also choose to take a moment to remember the past.

YOUR ACHIEVEMENTS

Have you ever taken the time to compile your accomplishments or achievements? Now is a great time to add them to your list. All of your achievements, big and small, personal and professional, count. Even adding little things to the list—like creating a delicious beef stroganoff or successfully clipping the cat's nails—will increase your pride. Also, add compliments or thanks that you receive. Reviewing your list can also be a source of inspiration for future achievements.

129

SUBJECTS OF INTEREST

Do you love learning new things? Did you love certain subjects in school and have you always discovered opportunities around you to learn more? Something that will bring you happiness is making a list of key facts and other things you learn about a subject (or subjects) you are really interested in. Choose subjects you are really interested in and start writing down key facts to add to your list.

MUSIC

Music stirs powerful emotions in all of us. Have you thought about how your favorite songs make you feel? How you felt when you realized that you are not the only person in the world to feel that way? When you haven't heard a favorite song in a while and you listen to it, what happens to your mood?

You can add favorite songs, maybe even describing how they make you feel, to your list. Are there events or people connected to these songs? Were you a certain age? Are they mainly positive/happy songs, or is there another theme?

Music is one of those powerful influences in our lives. Remember some of the songs that have affected you over the years. Whether jazz, hip-hop, country, or any other kind, few things can impact us like music.

ART

The School of Life, an organization in the United Kingdom dedicated to emotional intelligence, says that one way to conceive of what artists do is to think that they are, in their own way, running advertising campaigns. These "advertising campaigns" are not for anything expensive or usually even available for purchase, but for the many things that are of huge human importance and constantly in danger of being forgotten. The images created by artists can reawaken us to the genuine, but too-easily-forgotten value, of particular pieces of our lives.

So maybe David Hockney or Albrecht Dürer was "advertising" the beauty and value of trees or grass. These pictures make us realize the beauty of ordinary things and occasions. Art—images and photography, artwork, and what you see with your own eyes—honors the elusive but real value of ordinary life. Art teaches us to be grateful and make the best of our circumstances: a job we do not always love, the imperfections of age, our frustrated ambitions and our attempts to stay loyal to irritable but loved family members. Art can do the opposite of glamorize what we do not have or cannot attain. Art can reawaken us to the genuine merit of life. It is advertising for the things we really NEED. Add your favorite pieces to your list.

Changing Your Brain

Using awareness and savoring during each day can promote positive changes in your brain. You can cultivate happiness on your own, looking for the good in your everyday experiences and taking little opportunities to savor them and learn from those experiences.

LAUGHING

Make a list of the things that can always make you laugh.

Mindful laughter can be a form of meditation. When you laugh, you give yourself over to the immediacy of the present moment. You are also able to momentarily transcend minor physical and mental stresses. Practiced in the morning, laughing meditation can lend a joyful quality to the entire day. Practiced in the evening, laughing meditation is a potent relaxant that has been known to inspire pleasant dreams. Laughter can also help open your eyes to previously unnoticed absurdities that can make life seem less serious.

There are three stages to mindful laughter, and each one can last anywhere from five to twenty minutes. The first stage involves stretching your body like a cat and breathing deeply. Your stretch should start at the hands and feet before you move through the rest of your body. Stretch out the muscles in your face by yawning and making silly faces. The second stage of the meditation is pure laughter. Imagine a humorous situation, remember funny jokes, or think about how odd it is to be laughing by yourself. When the giggles start to rise, let them. Let the laughter ripple through your belly and down into the soles of your feet. Let the laughter lead to physical movement. Roll on the floor, if you have to, and keep on laughing until you stop. The final stage of the meditation is one of silence. Sit with your eyes closed and focus on your breath.

PETS

Do you have, or have you ever had, any pets? Journal about them or another animal you have known in regard to how they are simply, wholeheartedly themselves. Even though they may be asleep much of the time, they are always acutely aware of what's going on around them. Write about your gratitude for your creatures and their love.

MEDITATION

Sit in a comfortable position and let your eyes close gently. Invite your body to relax and ease into the ground or cushion. Let go and accept the non-doing of meditation. Sense and listen to your breath. Feel the air as it goes in and out of your nostrils. Feel the rise and fall of your chest and abdomen. Allow your attention to settle where you feel your breath most clearly. Keep following the breath. Allow it to be exactly as it is; do not control it. See the pause between breaths. Out of sheer habit, thoughts will arise. Just watch them as you would the cars of a train going by. See them, acknowledge them, let them go, and come back to the breath. It does not matter how many times you get caught up in a thought, or for how long. Begin again and bring awareness back to the breath. If a physical sensation arises, watch it the same way that you would watch your thoughts. This is your practice. You are strengthening mindfulness. Awareness of one whole in-breath and one whole out-breath is a big accomplishment. For twenty minutes, follow your breath with singular attention. As you gently open your eyes, try to carry the momentum of your mindfulness into your next activity.

Find a way to work meditation into your schedule for the next week. Note how you feel before and after each session.

DATE:

BEFORE THE SESSION

AFTER THE SESSION

DATE:

BEFORE THE SESSION

AFTER THE SESSION

DATE:

BEFORE THE SESSION

AFTER THE SESSION

DATE:

BEFORE THE SESSION

AFTER THE SESSION

DATE:

BEFORE THE SESSION

AFTER THE SESSION

DATE:

BEFORE THE SESSION

AFTER THE SESSION

DATE:

BEFORE THE SESSION

AFTER THE SESSION

How did it go? What did you learn about yourself?

VISUALIZATION

Imagine that you are a ball of light—clear, luminous, pure, and perfect. Envision a golden sun in your heart, which opens like a sunflower. Give warmth and light to all who wander through the darkness of ignorance and delusion. Awaken spiritual awareness and joy like the dawn. Let go and see the afterglow. Simply relax in the joy and peace of this visualization.

Find a way to work visualization into your schedule for the next week. Note how you feel before and after each session.

DATE:

BEFORE THE SESSION

AFTER THE SESSION

DATE:

BEFORE THE SESSION

AFTER THE SESSION

DATE:

BEFORE THE SESSION

AFTER THE SESSION

DATE:

BEFORE THE SESSION

AFTER THE SESSION

DATE:

BEFORE THE SESSION

AFTER THE SESSION

DATE:

BEFORE THE SESSION

AFTER THE SESSION

DATE:

BEFORE THE SESSION

AFTER THE SESSION

How did it go? What did you learn about yourself?

MEDIA REDUCTION PLAN

Spend the next week making a log of every time you engage with electronic and broadcast media during the day, and what it is.

DATE

MEDIA

DATE

MEDIA

DATE

MEDIA

DATE

MEDIA

10100

1001001

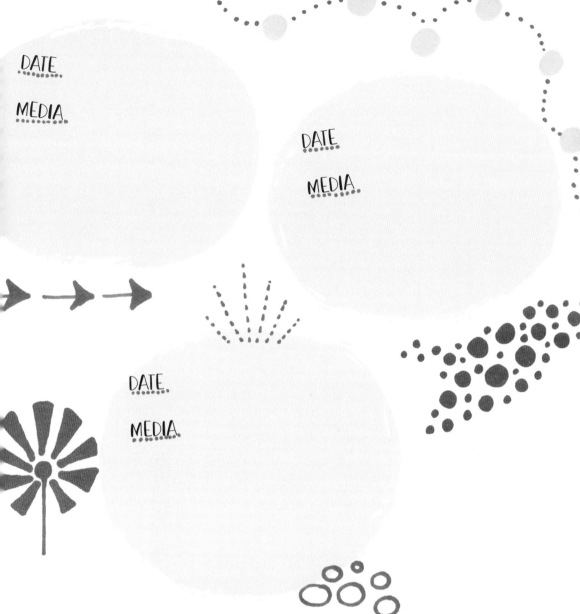

DATE.

MEDIA

DATE

MEDIA.

DATE.

MEDIA.

Is this the right amount for you?

Challenge yourself to go on a media reduction plan. It can include listening to radio and music, using your phone, online activity, watching television, and the like. It is an experiment in restorative solitude that explores the importance of quiet time for clarity, creativity, and spirituality. How did it go?

Choose a small way of cutting down on your screen time going forward. For example, put your devices away before mealtime, create some tech-free zones in your home, limit news consumption to once a day, or limit social media.

BELONGING

The sense of belonging is a basic need and part of the answer to the eternal question: Who am I? You belong to a family, a group, a society, and a profession, and these affiliations define you and give you reasons for existing. We come to know who we are by our reference to others. Write your name in the box below, and mind map your connections to different communities and important people. For example, you could draw a branch off of the box to indicate family, and another to indicate your church community.

GIVING BACK

What are ten ways you could improve the well-being of people, animals, the environment, your community, and/or the world?

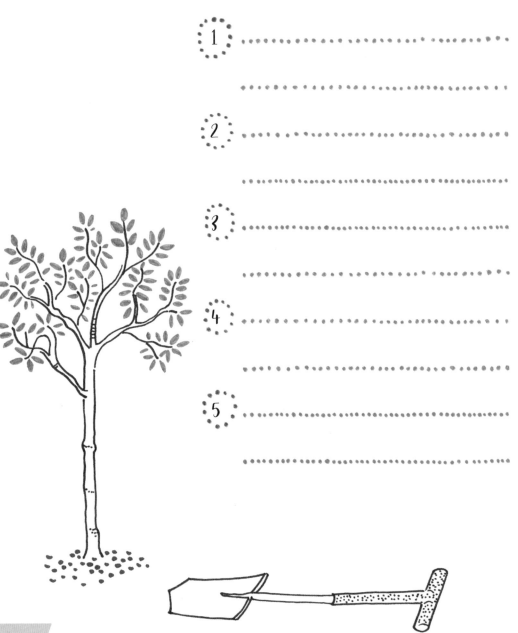

1 ....

....

2 ....

....

3 ....

....

4 ....

....

5 ....

....

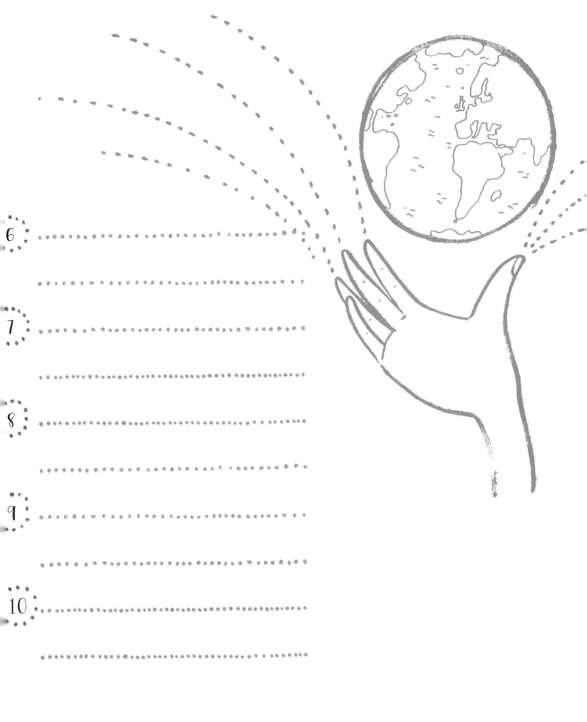

6 ....

....

7 ....

....

8 ....

....

9 ....

....

10 ....

....

Pick one or two of the items on your list and get started on them.

Sharing Happiness

Look at happiness as an unlimited supply that you can share and receive. It is your privilege to use your joy and to share it. To your happiness diary, add ways you can give/share happiness with others. You can start with family members and friends, and then extend to the whole world.

EXPRESSING FEELINGS

WHO ARE THE PEOPLE WHO ARE THE MOST IMPORTANT TO YOU?

DO THEY KNOW HOW YOU FEEL?
PICK ONE AND MAKE A PLAN TO LET THAT PERSON KNOW.

Is there someone you want
to ask for forgiveness,
even if it's been years?
Why? Make a plan to ask.

WORTH COMPLIMENTING

Make a list of nice things you could say to people. By training yourself to think of nice things to say, you'll always be able to pull them out when they're relevant.

WHY YOU'RE GREAT

Pick one friend. Make a top-ten list of reasons why you think he or she is great. Share this list with that person.

1 ....

....

2 ....

....

3 ....

....

4 ....

....

5 ....

....

6 ....

....

7 ....

....

8 ....

....

9 ....

....

10 ....

....

LOVE LETTER

Today, write a love letter straight from the heart. There are many different types of love you can feel, so don't limit it just to a spouse or significant other—and the person can be alive or dead. Write about what you most love and appreciate about this person. If you want to, send him or her a copy.

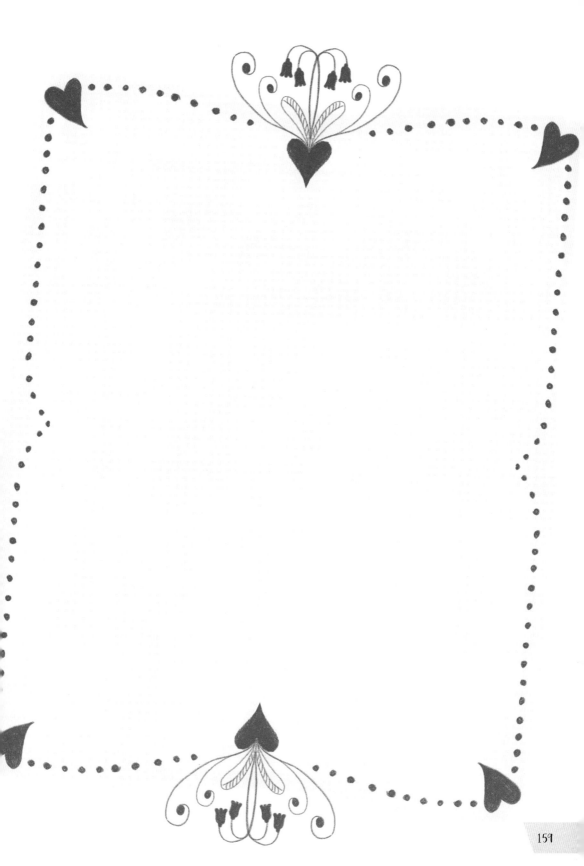

ABOUT THE AUTHOR

Author of the bestseller *14,000 Things to be Happy About,* Barbara Ann Kipfer has written more than 75 books and calendars of wit and inspiration, thesauri and dictionaries, trivia and question books, archaeology reference, and happiness and spiritually themed books. Kipfer is a professional lexicographer and holds Ph.D.s in linguistics, archaeology, and Buddhist studies.